Language Lessons *for* Children

BY KATHY WEITZ

PRIMER ONE AUTUMN
STUDENT BOOK

Acknowledgements

Although my name is on the cover, the Primer series in many ways has been a collaborative effort. I owe a great debt of gratitude to many folks. The gorgeous cover designs are the craftsmanship of my friend Jayme Metzgar, with image credit to The Graphics Fairy (www.thegraphicsfairy.com). Many other friends have helped with both editing and content: in particular, Kimberlynn Curles, Emily Cook, Cheryl Turner, Karen Gill, Carolyn Vance, Lene Jaqua and the exceptional teachers, moms, and students of Providence Preparatory Academy. And of course, the main source of help and encouragement in myriad ways—from design consultation to field testing to dinner duty—has come from my dear husband and my wonderful children.

~kpw

© COPYRIGHT 2014. KATHY WEITZ
COTTAGE PRESS
WWW.COTTAGEPRESS.NET

Printed in the United States of America.

All rights reserved. This book or any portion thereof may not be reproduced or used in any manner whatsoever without the express written permission of the publisher except for the use of brief quotations in a book review.

Primer One Autumn
Contents

Materials Needed for *Primer One Autumn* vi

Week 1 3
Solomon Grundy
Days of the Week
Phonograms **ay** *and* **a** *at the end of a word*

Week 2 13
from THE TALE OF SQUIRREL NUTKIN
Making Plurals
Making Past Tense
Days of the Week
Rhyming Words
Making Past Tense & Plural

Week 3 23
from JUST A HAPPY DAY
Making Past Tense & Plural
Rhyming Words
Phonogram **or** *after* **w**
Days of the Week & Abbreviations

Week 4 33
Jesus, Tender Shepherd
Phonogram **ea**
Words with Silent Letters
Days of the Week
Making Past Tense & Plural

Week 5 43
from EEYORE LOSES A TAIL AND POOH FINDS ONE
Phonogram **ou**
Rhyming Words
Adding Suffixes to One Syllable Words
Making Plural

Week 6 53

Autumn

Phonogram **ow**
Adding Suffixes to One Syllable Words
Rhyming Words

Week 7 63

from The Jubilate Deo

Making Compound words with "Full"
Making Plural
Adding Suffixes to Words Ending with a Silent **-e**
Rhyming Words

Week 8 73

from Land

The Days of the Week
Adding Suffixes to One-Syllable Words
Adding Suffixes to Words Ending with a Silent **-e**
Adding Suffixes

Week 9 83

from All People That On Earth Do Dwell

Phonogram **oi**
Making Past Tense
Rhyming Words

Week 10 93

from All People That on Earth Do Dwell

Adding Suffixes
Phonogram **oo**
Rhyming Words

Week 11 103

from The Gospel of Luke

Homonyms
Adding Suffixes
Making Past Tense
Days of the Week

Week 12 113

Away in a Manger

Making Past Tense
Rhyming Words
Phonograms **ee** *and* **ea**
Homonyms

Materials Needed for Primer One Autumn

All materials, resources, and links listed below are available at Cottage Press:
www.cottagepress.net

Required

- **Primer One Teaching Helps** ~ Required to effectively teach all lessons in in Primer. This one book contains teaching helps for all three Primer One student books. It contains instructions for all nature study and picture study lessons, tips and notes for teaching the Spelling, Grammar, and Word Usage lessons, and an answer key for the exercises that warrant it. Teach each lesson in Primer with this book open for ready reference.

- **Primer Resources Webpage** ~ Linked from *cottagepress.net* with many resources for nature and picture study. Bookmark this webpage.

- **Picture Study PDFs** ~ Free, downloadable PDFs for individual artists that include images of selected paintings along with biographical notes and links to many online resources. Available artists include: Audubon, Bruegel, Cassatt, DaVinci, Delacroix, Durer, Homer, Michelangelo, Millet, Monet, Rembrandt, Renoir, Rubens, Stuart, Titian, Van Eyck, Van Gogh, Vermeer. The *Primer Resources Webpage* has links to these free PDFs.

- **The Aesop for Children, illustrated by Milo Winter** ~ Aesop's fables retold in simple, elegant prose for children with beautiful full-color illustrations. This classic edition will delight all ages. All narration selections for *Primer One Autumn* are found in this book. Purchase this from the Cottage Press bookstore or download it for free from Project Gutenberg as a PDF or ebook.

    http://www.gutenberg.org/ebooks/19994

- **A Systematic Phonics and Spelling Program** ~ The lessons in the *Primer* books are designed to reinforce phonics and spelling rules taught in such a program. See recommendations on the *Primer Resources Webpage*.

Optional

- **High quality colored pencils** ~ Prismacolors by Berol are wonderful!

- **Books and Resources for the nature and picture study lessons** ~ Links to resources (both free and for purchase) are available on the *Primer Resources Webpage*. Check your local library also.

WEEKLY LESSONS

Drawing Page

Solomon Grundy

Solomon Grundy,

Born on Monday,

Christened on Tuesday,

Married on Wednesday,

Took ill on Thursday,

Worse on Friday,

Died on Saturday,

Buried on Sunday:

This is the end

Of Solomon Grundy.

—TRADITIONAL ENGLISH NURSERY RHYME

Week 1 • Day 1

Today is _____
　　　　　　Day　　　　　　　　Date　　　　　　　　Year

READ AND NARRATE

The Young Crab and His Mother
The Aesop for Children, illustrated by Milo Winter

Vocabulary to study before you read:

world	straight	forward
answered	obediently	learn
sideways	example	

Draw a picture or series of pictures illustrating the story.

Week 1 ♦ Day 1

COPYBOOK

Solomon Grundy,

Born on Monday,

Christened on Tuesday,

Married on Wednesday,

_____

_____

_____

DAYS OF THE WEEK

When you practice spelling the days of the week, it is helpful to "think to spell" them by syllables, even though you may not pronounce them that way. For example, say to yourself, "Wed NES Day" as you spell Wednesday.

Mon · day

_____

Tu · es · day

_____

Wed · nes · day

_____

Refer to Teaching Helps for further explanation.

Week 1 • Day 2

Today is _____
　　　　　　　Day　　　　　　　　Date　　　　　　　　Year

NATURE STUDY

*Find out what direction your house faces. Write **N** for North, **S** for South, **E** for East, and **W** for West on the drawing below.*

BACK OF YOUR HOUSE

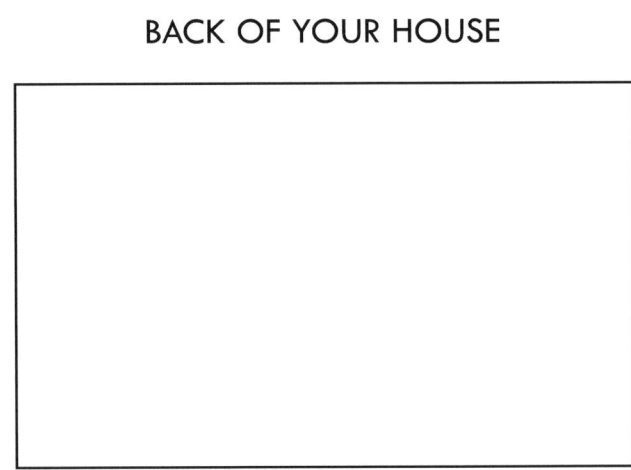

FRONT OF YOUR HOUSE

Learn this mnemonic to remember the order of the directions:

Never **E**at **S**hredded **W**heat

*Begin by pointing North - say **N**ever*

*Do a 1/4 turn clockwise, or to your right - say **E**at*

*Another 1/4 turn clockwise, or to your right - say **S**hredded*

*Another 1/4 turn clockwise, or to your right - say **W**heat*

Week 1 • Day 2

COPYBOOK

Took ill on Thursday,

Worse on Friday,

Died on Saturday,

DAYS OF THE WEEK

Remember to pronounce each syllable as you spell.

Thurs · day

Fri · day

Sat · ur · day

Sun · day

Week 1 • Day 3

Today is _____
                              Day   Date   Year

READ AND NARRATE

The Frogs and the Ox
The Aesop for Children, illustrated by Milo Winter

Vocabulary to study before you read:

splashed	heavily	crushed
puffing	monster	burst
attempt	impossible	

Draw a picture or series of pictures illustrating the story.

COPYBOOK

Buried on Sunday:

This is the end

Of Solomon Grundy.

DAYS OF THE WEEK

Write the days of the week below.

Sunday

Monday

Tuesday

Wednesday

Thursday

Friday

Saturday

Week 1 • Day 4

Today is _____
　　　　　　　　Day　　　　　　　　Date　　　　　　　　Year

PICTURE STUDY

In the space above, make your own rendering of the current work of art using colored pencils, or paste a printout from the Picture Study PDF. Write the title and date of the work on one line and the artist's name on the line below it.

DICTATION

PHONOGRAMS **AY** AND **A** AT THE END OF A WORD

Words that say /ā/ at the end usually end in **ay**. *If a word ends with* **a**, *it usually says* /**ah**/.

Read these words, then copy them.

away	railway	zebra
play	birthday	umbrella
gray	stray	soda

DRAWING PAGE

from THE TALE OF SQUIRREL NUTKIN

One autumn when the nuts were ripe, and the leaves on the hazel bushes were golden and green—Nutkin and Twinkleberry and all the other little squirrels came out of the wood, and down to the edge of the lake.

They made little rafts out of twigs, and they paddled away over the water to Owl Island to gather nuts.

Each squirrel had a little sack and a large oar, and spread out his tail for a sail.

—BEATRIX POTTER

Week 2 ♦ Day 1

Today is _____
　　　　　　Day　　　　　　　Date　　　　　　　Year

READ AND NARRATE

Belling the Cat
The Aesop for Children, illustrated by Milo Winter

Vocabulary to study before you read:

enemy	knowing	constant
claws	hardly	discussed
successful	immediately	surprised
thought	rejoicing	fortune

Draw a picture or series of pictures illustrating the story.

COPYBOOK

One autumn when the nuts were ripe, and the leaves on the hazel bushes were golden and green—Nutkin and Twinkleberry and all the other little squirrels came out of the wood, and down to the edge of the lake.

MAKING PLURALS

Most names of persons, places, things, or ideas are made plural (more than one) by adding **-s** *or* **-es** *to the base word. There are several words in this lesson that end with an* **f**. *In these words, the* **f** *changes to* **v** *and then you add* **-es**.

Example: **leaf**, *change* **f → v + es = leaves**

Make these words plural.

nut	wish	loaf
wood	sash	sheaf
lake	marsh	knife

WEEK 2 • DAY 2

Today is _____
 Day   Date   Year

NATURE STUDY

*Draw a picture of what you see when you look out of a window on the **north** side of your house.*

Keep practicing your compass directions as you ride in the car this week. Find out what direction you are traveling and then figure out the other directions from that.

COPYBOOK

They made little rafts out of twigs, and they paddled away over the water to Owl Island to gather nuts.

MAKING PAST TENSE

*The past tense ending, **-ed**, added to an action word (a verb), tells us the action happened in the past. It says /**d**/ or /**t**/ unless the word ends in **-d** or **-t**, and then it says /**ed**/.*

Sometimes the past tense is formed by totally changing the word.

   Example: **have → had**

Make these words past tense.

gather	land	come
call	plant	have
row	lift	am
fill	pick	tell

Week 2 • Day 3

Today is _____
            Day   Date   Year

READ AND NARRATE

The Boy and the Filberts
The Aesop for Children, illustrated by Milo Winter

Vocabulary to study before you read:

permission	filberts	fistful
unwilling	vexed	disappointed
satisfied	attempt	

Draw a picture or series of pictures illustrating the story.

COPYBOOK

Each squirrel had a little sack and a large oar, and spread out his tail for a sail.

DAYS OF THE WEEK

Sunday

Monday

Tuesday

Wednesday

Thursday

Friday

Saturday

RHYMING WORDS

Write three words that rhyme with **sail**.

Week 2 • Day 4

Today is _____
                Day   Date   Year

PICTURE STUDY

DICTATION

_____

_____

_____

_____

_____

_____

_____

_____

MAKING PAST TENSE & PLURAL

Make these words past tense.

get	sing	hunt
pull	make	take

Make these words plural.

| bush | leaf | oar |

DRAWING PAGE

from JUST A HAPPY DAY

"After all," Anne had said to Marilla once, "I believe the nicest and sweetest days are not those on which anything very splendid or wonderful or exciting happens but just those that bring simple little pleasures, following one another softly, like pearls slipping off a string."

Life at Green Gables was full of just such days, for Anne's adventures and misadventures, like those of other people, did not all happen at once, but were sprinkled over the year, with long stretches of harmless, happy days between, filled with work and dreams and laughter and lessons. Such a day came late in August. In the forenoon Anne and Diana rowed the delighted twins down the pond to the sandshore to pick "sweet grass" and paddle in the surf, over which the wind was harping an old lyric learned when the world was young.

—*ANNE OF AVONLEA*, BY LUCY MAUDE MONTGOMERY

Week 3 ♦ Day 1

Today is _____
                Day   Date   Year

READ AND NARRATE

The Town Mouse and the Country Mouse
The Aesop for Children, illustrated by Milo Winter

Vocabulary to study before you read:

visited	relative	sparingly
polite	listened	hedgerow
luxuries	delights	leavings
delicious	scurried	prefer
security	poverty	uncertainty

Draw a picture or series of pictures illustrating the story.

COPYBOOK

"After all," Anne had said to Marilla once, "I believe the nicest and sweetest days are not those on which anything very splendid or wonderful or exciting happens but just those that bring simple little pleasures, following one another softly, like pearls slipping off a string."

MAKING PAST TENSE & PLURAL

Make these words past tense.

are	bring	follow
do	come	learn

Make these words plural.

pearl   stretch   lyric

Week 3 ♦ Day 2

Today is _____
　　　　　　　Day　　　　　　　Date　　　　　　　Year

NATURE STUDY

*Draw a picture of what you see when you look out of a window on the **east** side of your house.*

Keep practicing your directions. Do you know what direction you travel from home to get to the post office? to the playground? to church?

COPYBOOK

Life at Green Gables was full of just such days, for Anne's adventures and misadventures, like those of other people, did not all happen at once, but were sprinkled over the year, with long stretches of harmless, happy days between, filled with work and dreams and laughter and lessons.

RHYMING WORDS

Write three words that rhyme with **work.**

Write three words that rhyme with **days.**

Week 3 • Day 3

Today is _____
               Day   Date   Year

READ AND NARRATE

The Fox and the Grapes
The Aesop for Children, illustrated by Milo Winter

Vocabulary to study before you read:

spied	trained	watered
gazed	vain	disgust
sour	scornfully	despise
belittle		

Draw a picture or series of pictures illustrating the story.

COPYBOOK

Such a day came late in August. In the forenoon Anne and Diana rowed the delighted twins down the pond to the sandshore to pick "sweet grass" and paddle in the surf, over which the wind was harping an old lyric learned when the world was young.

PHONOGRAM **OR** AFTER **W**

The phonogram **or** *usually says* /**er**/ *when it comes after* **w**.

Make these **or** *words plural.*

world   work   word

worm   firework   silkworm

Week 3 • Day 4

Today is _____
                    Day   Date   Year

PICTURE STUDY

Week 3 • Day 4

DICTATION

DAYS OF THE WEEK & ABBREVIATIONS

The days of the week can be abbreviated (shortened) by writing the first three letters followed by a period. Write the days of the week, and beside each day, write its abbreviation.

Sunday

Monday

Tuesday

Wednesday

Thursday

Friday

Saturday

DRAWING PAGE

JESUS, TENDER SHEPHERD

Jesus, tender Shepherd, hear me;

Bless Thy little lamb tonight:

Through the darkness be Thou near me,

Keep me safe till morning light.

All this day Thy hand has led me,

And I thank Thee for Thy care;

Thou has warmed me, clothed, and fed me;

Listen to my evening prayer.

Let my sins be all forgiven;

Bless the friends I love so well:

Take us all at last to heaven,

Happy there with Thee to dwell. Amen.

—MARY DUNCAN

Week 4 • Day 1

Today is _____
　　　　　　Day　　　　　Date　　　　　Year

READ AND NARRATE

The Bundle of Sticks
The Aesop for Children, illustrated by Milo Winter

Vocabulary to study before you read:

certain	quarreling	striking
discord	misfortune	violent
moping	surly	untied
impossible	injure	unity

Draw a picture or series of pictures illustrating the story.

COPYBOOK

Jesus, tender Shepherd, hear me;

Bless Thy little lamb tonight:

Through the darkness be Thou near me,

Keep me safe till morning light.

PHONOGRAM EA

The phonogram **ea** *can say /ē/ as in* **tea**, */ĕ/ as in* **head**, *or /ā/ as in* **steak**.

Read these words, then copy them.

hear	heaven	bear
near	meadow	wear
each	bread	great

Week 4 • Day 2

Today is _____
      Day   Date   Year

NATURE STUDY

*Draw a picture of what you see when you look out of a window on the **south** side of your house.*

Keep practicing your directions. Do you know what direction you travel to get to your grandparents' house?

COPYBOOK

All this day Thy hand has led me,

And I thank Thee for thy care;

Thou has warmed me, clothed, and fed me;

Listen to my evening prayer.

WORDS WITH SILENT LETTERS

Some words have a silent **t**, *like* **listen**. *It helps to "think to spell" these words by syllables, so that when you are spelling* **listen**, *you say* **lis-ten**, *pronouncing the /t/ sound as you write it. Practice pronouncing the silent letter as you spell these words.*

| listen | soften | fasten |

| castle | nestle | hasten |

When **b** *or an* **n** *comes after m, they are usually silent. "Think to spell" these words.*

| lamb | autumn | crumb |

Week 4 • Day 3

Today is _____
                       Day   Date   Year

READ AND NARRATE

The Oxen and the Wheels
The Aesop for Children, illustrated by Milo Winter

Vocabulary to study before you read:

drawing	miry	complain
compared	creaked	groaned
complaining	endure	weights
suffer	least	

Draw a picture or series of pictures illustrating the story.

Week 4 • Day 3

COPYBOOK

Let my sins be all forgiven;

Bless the friends I love so well:

Take us all at last to heaven,

Happy there with Thee to dwell. Amen.

DAYS OF THE WEEK

Write the days of the week and their abbreviations.

Week 4 • Day 4

Today is _____
         Day   Date   Year

PICTURE STUDY

DICTATION

MAKING PAST TENSE & PLURAL

Make these words past tense.

hear	thank	listen

take	hasten	keep

Make these words plural.

hand	church	elf

DRAWING PAGE

from Eeyore Loses a Tail and Pooh Finds One

So Winnie-the-Pooh went off to find Eeyore's tail.

It was a fine spring morning in the forest as he started out. Little soft clouds played happily in a blue sky, skipping from time to time in front of the sun as if they had come to put it out, and then sliding away suddenly so that the next might have his turn. Through them and between them the sun shone bravely; and a copse which had worn its firs all the year round seemed old and dowdy now beside the new green lace which the beeches had put on so prettily.

—*WINNIE-THE-POOH*, BY A. A. MILNE

Week 5 • Day 1

Today is _____
          Day   Date   Year

READ AND NARRATE

The Lion and the Mouse
The Aesop for Children, illustrated by Milo Winter

Vocabulary to study before you read:

timid	unexpectedly	fright
haste	roused	angrily
creature	amused	generous
stalking	prey	gnawed

Draw a picture or series of pictures illustrating the story.

COPYBOOK

So Winnie-the-Pooh went off to find Eeyore's tail.

It was a fine spring morning in the forest as he started out.

PHONOGRAM **OU**

*The phonogram **ou** can say /**ow**/ as in **shout**, /ō/ as in **four**, or /**oo**/ as in **soup**, or /ŭ/ as in **young**.*

Read these words, then copy them.

out	pour	wound (/ow/ sound)
cloud	soul	wound (/oo/ sound)
house	you	touch

RHYMING WORDS

*Write three words that rhyme with **out**.*

Week 5 • Day 2

Today is _____
             Day   Date   Year

NATURE STUDY

*Draw a picture of what you see when you look out of a window on the **west** side of your house.*

Keep practicing your directions. What direction do you travel to go to the grocery store?

COPYBOOK

Little soft clouds played happily in a blue sky, skipping from time to time in front of the sun as if they had come to put it out, and then sliding away suddenly so that the next might have his turn.

ADDING SUFFIXES TO ONE SYLLABLE WORDS

*To add a suffix that begins with a vowel to a one-syllable word, double the final consonant IF the word ends in one vowel followed by one consonant that you can see AND hear. (When a word ends in **x**, how many consonants do you HEAR?)*

Add -ing to these words.

skip	get	play
put	sin	box
ship	beg	blow

Week 5 • Day 3

Today is _____
                Day   Date   Year

READ AND NARRATE

The Shepherd Boy and the Wolf
The Aesop for Children, illustrated by Milo Winter

Vocabulary to study before you read:

tended	pasture	dull
Villagers	expected	excitement
laughter	creeping	terror
liars	believed	truth

Draw a picture or series of pictures illustrating the story.

COPYBOOK

Through them and between them the sun shone bravely; and a copse which had worn its firs all the year round seemed old and dowdy now beside the new green lace which the beeches had put on so prettily.

ADDING SUFFIXES TO ONE SYLLABLE WORDS

To add a suffix that begins with a vowel to a one-syllable word, double the final consonant IF the word ends in one vowel followed by one consonant that you can see AND hear.

*Add **-ed** to these words.*

skip	beg	play
ship	bag	box
sin	stop	row

Week 5 • Day 4

Today is _____
             Day   Date   Year

PICTURE STUDY

DICTATION

MAKING PLURAL

Make these words plural.

tail	spring	morning
cloud	green	beech
grass	match	hoof

DRAWING PAGE

Autumn

The morns are meeker than they were,
The nuts are getting brown;
The berry's cheek is plumper,
The rose is out of town.

The maple wears a gayer scarf,
The field a scarlet gown.
Lest I should be old fashioned,
I'll put a trinket on.

—EMILY DICKINSON

Week 6 • Day 1

Today is _____
　　　　　　　Day　　　　　　　　　　　　　Date　　　　　　　　　　　　　Year

READ AND NARRATE

The Plane Tree
The Aesop for Children, illustrated by Milo Winter

Vocabulary to study before you read:

*travellers	shade	widespreading
pleasant	useless	litter
ungrateful	receive	blessings
least	appreciated	

*British spelling

Draw a picture or series of pictures illustrating the story.

COPYBOOK

The morns are meeker than they were,

The nuts are getting brown;

The berry's cheek is plumper,

The rose is out of town.

PHONOGRAM OW

The phonogram **ow** *can say* /**ow**/ *as in* **cow**, *or* /**ō**/ *as in* **snow**.

Read these words, then copy them.

town	growl	grown
brown	clown	window
how	row	bowl

Week 6 ♦ Day 2

Today is _____
                Day   Date   Year

NATURE STUDY

Tree Observation: Draw the leaf and the seed of the tree you are observing.

[ ]

Identify the tree, and write its name:

COPYBOOK

The maple wears a gayer scarf,

The field a scarlet gown.

Lest I should be old fashioned,

I'll put a trinket on.

ADDING SUFFIXES TO ONE SYLLABLE WORDS

To add a suffix that begins with a vowel to a one-syllable word, double the final consonant if the word ends in one vowel followed by one consonant that you can see AND hear.

Add **-er** to these words.

skip	zip	gay
ship	big	box
sin	stop	row
flip	meek	plump

Week 6 • Day 3

Today is _____
                         Day   Date   Year

READ AND NARRATE

The Farmer and the Stork
The Aesop for Children, illustrated by Milo Winter

Vocabulary to study before you read:

trusting	nature	dismally
entangled	meshes	spare
character	thieving	punishment
judged	company	

Draw a picture or series of pictures illustrating the story.

COPYBOOK

The morns are meeker than they were,

The nuts are getting brown;

The berry's cheek is plumper,

The rose is out of town.

The maple wears a gayer scarf,

The field a scarlet gown.

Lest I should be old fashioned,

I'll put a trinket on.

Week 6 • Day 4

Today is _____
              Day   Date   Year

PICTURE STUDY

DICTATION

RHYMING WORDS

Write three words that rhyme with **town**.

Write three words that rhyme with **were**.

Write three words that rhyme with **rose**.

DRAWING PAGE

from THE JUBILATE DEO

Make a joyful shout to the Lord, all you lands!
Serve the Lord with gladness;
> Come before His presence with singing.

Know that the Lord, He is God;
> It is He who has made us, and not we ourselves;
> We are His people and the sheep of His pasture.

Enter into His gates with thanksgiving,
> And into His courts with praise.
> Be thankful to Him, and bless His name.

—PSALM 100:1-4, NEW KING JAMES VERSION

Week 7 • Day 1

Today is _____
　　　　　　　Day　　　　　　　　　　Date　　　　　　　　　　Year

READ AND NARRATE

The Oak and the Reeds
The Aesop for Children, illustrated by Milo Winter

Vocabulary to study before you read:

slender	mournful	complain
slightest	ruffles	surface
bow	strength	hurricane
yielding	redoubled	folly
resist	stubbornly	destroyed

Draw a picture or series of pictures illustrating the story.

COPYBOOK

Make a joyful shout to the Lord, all you lands!

Serve the Lord with gladness;

Come before His presence with singing.

MAKING COMPOUND WORDS WITH "FULL"

When **full** *is added to another word to make a new compound word, it is spelled with just one* **l**.

joy + full =	(full of joy)
thank + full =	(full of thanks)
hope + full =	(full of hope)
rest + full =	(full of rest)
help + full =	(full of help)
peace + full =	(full of peace)
grace + full =	(full of grace)

Week 7 • Day 2

Today is _____
　　　　　　　Day　　　　　　　　　Date　　　　　　　　Year

NATURE STUDY

Tree Observation: Draw the leaf and the seed of the tree you are observing.

Identify the tree, and write its name:

COPYBOOK

Know that the Lord, He is God;

It is He who has made us, and not we ourselves;

We are His people and the sheep of His pasture.

MAKING PLURAL

Make these words plural.

people	sheep	self
court	land	shout
I	name	pasture
calf	fox	deer

Week 7 • Day 3

Today is _____
   Day   Date   Year

READ AND NARRATE

The Boys and the Frogs
The Aesop for Children, illustrated by Milo Winter

Vocabulary to study before you read:

amused	throwing	skip
trembling	bravest	cruel
cause	unhappiness	

Draw a picture or series of pictures illustrating the story.

COPYBOOK

Enter into His gates with thanksgiving,

    And into His courts with praise.

    Be thankful to Him, and bless His name.

ADDING SUFFIXES TO WORDS ENDING WITH A SILENT -E

*Words that end with a silent **-e** drop the **e** when adding a suffix that begins with a vowel.*

*Add the suffix **-ing** to these words.*

make	serve	praise
give	name	pasture
love	please	paddle

Week 7 • Day 4

Today is _____
                Day   Date   Year

PICTURE STUDY

DICTATION

_____

_____

_____

_____

_____

_____

_____

_____

_____

_____

RHYMING WORDS

Write three words that rhyme with **know**.

_____

Write three words that rhyme with **singing**.

_____

DRAWING PAGE

from LAND

At daybreak one cold November morning, a glad shout rang through the ship. "Land! Land!"

Yes, there lay the land—that new land which was to be their home and ours.

There were no rocky cliffs like those of England. Before them rose tall, green pine trees, and great oaks still wearing their dress of reddish brown.

Not a town or a single house could they see. No smoke rose from the forest to tell them where a village lay hidden. Not a sound was heard but the whistling of the cold wind through the ropes and masts, and the lapping of the water about the boat.

—*Stories of the Pilgrims,* by Margaret Pumphrey

Week 8 • Day 1

Today is _____
                      Day   Date   Year

READ AND NARRATE

The Ants and the Grasshopper
The Aesop for Children, illustrated by Milo Winter

Vocabulary to study before you read:

autumn	bustling	stored
humbly	shrugged	disgust

Draw a picture or series of pictures illustrating the story.

COPYBOOK

At daybreak one cold November morning, a glad shout rang through the ship. "Land! Land!"

Yes, there lay the land—that new land which was to be their home and ours.

THE DAYS OF THE WEEK

Week 8 • Day 2

Today is _____
                   Day   Date   Year

NATURE STUDY

Tree Observation: Draw the leaf and the seed of the tree you are observing.

Identify the tree, and write its name:

COPYBOOK

There were no rocky cliffs like those of England. Before them rose tall, green pine trees, and great oaks still wearing their dress of reddish brown.

ADDING SUFFIXES TO ONE-SYLLABLE WORDS

To add a suffix that begins with a vowel to a one-syllable word, double the final consonant IF the word ends in one vowel followed by one consonant that you can see AND hear.

Add endings to these words:

red + -er   red + -est   red + -ish

mad + -er   mad + -est   mad + ly

lap + -ed   lap + -ing   lap + -full

Week 8 • Day 3

Today is _____
         Day   Date   Year

READ AND NARRATE

The Two Goats
The Aesop for Children, illustrated by Milo Winter

Vocabulary to study before you read:

frisking	gayly	steeps
chasm	torrent	pride
permit	yield	misfortune
stubbornness		

Draw a picture or series of pictures illustrating the story.

COPYBOOK

    Not a town or a single house could they see. No smoke rose from the forest to tell them where a village lay hidden. Not a sound was heard but the whistling of the cold wind through the ropes and masts, and the lapping of the water about the boat.

ADDING SUFFIXES TO WORDS ENDING WITH A SILENT -E

Words that end with a silent -e drop the e when adding a suffix beginning with a vowel.

Add the suffix **-ing** *to these words.*

smoke   whistle   hide

Make these words past tense by adding **-ed**.

smoke   whistle   force

Week 8 • Day 4

Today is _____
　　　　　　　Day　　　　　　　　　Date　　　　　　　　　Year

PICTURE STUDY

DICTATION

___

ADDING SUFFIXES

Practice the rules you have learned for adding suffixes.

| plan + er | plan + ing | land + ing |

| sing + er | hid + en | whistle + er |

| nice + er | smoke + y | wind + y |

DRAWING PAGE

from All People That On Earth Do Dwell

All people that on earth do dwell,

Sing to the Lord with cheerful voice;

Him serve with fear, His praise forthtell,

Come ye before Him and rejoice.

The Lord, ye know, is God indeed;

Without our aid He did us make;

We are His folk, He doth us feed,

And for His sheep He doth us take.

—WILLIAM KETHE, 1561 (BASED ON PSALM 100)

Week 9 • Day 1

Today is _____
         Day   Date   Year

READ AND NARRATE

The Stag and His Reflection
The Aesop for Children, illustrated by Milo Winter

Vocabulary to study before you read:

crystal	mirrored	graceful
ashamed	spindly	cursed
magnificent	perceived	useless
ornaments	despise	

Draw a picture or series of pictures illustrating the story.

COPYBOOK

All people that on earth do dwell,

Sing to the Lord with cheerful voice;

Him serve with fear, His praise forthtell,

Come ye before Him and rejoice.

PHONOGRAM OI

*The phonogram **oi** cannot be used at the end of a word because English words do not end in **i**. Use **oy** at the end of a word, and sometimes in the middle.*

Read these words, then copy them.

| oil | voice | rejoice |

| boy | joy | enjoy |

| noise | spoil | loyal |

Week 9 • Day 2

Today is _____
  Day   Date   Year

NATURE STUDY

Discuss these the characteristics of mammals:

- ✓ have a backbone (vertebrates)
- ✓ are warm-blooded
- ✓ have lungs that breathe air
- ✓ have hair
- ✓ most give birth to live young
- ✓ feed their young with milk

List ten mammals below.

1. _____
2. _____
3. _____
4. _____
5. _____
6. _____
7. _____
8. _____
9. _____
10. _____

COPYBOOK

The Lord, ye know, is God indeed;

Without our aid He did us make;

We are His folk, He doth us feed,

And for His sheep He doth us take.

MAKING PAST TENSE

Make these words past tense. Remember the rules for adding suffixes.

do	sing	praise
is	come	rejoice
feed	are	take

Week 9 • Day 3

Today is _____
                         Day   Date   Year

READ AND NARRATE

The Dog and His Master's Dinner
The Aesop for Children, illustrated by Milo Winter

Vocabulary to study before you read:

learned	faithful	duty
tempted	discovered	attempts
argue	temptation	

Draw a picture or series of pictures illustrating the story.

COPYBOOK

All people that on earth do dwell,

Sing to the Lord with cheerful voice;

Him serve with fear, His praise forthtell,

Come ye before Him and rejoice.

The Lord, ye know, is God indeed;

Without our aid He did us make;

We are His folk, He doth us feed,

And for His sheep He doth us take.

Week 9 • Day 4

Today is _____
　　　　　　　Day　　　　　　　Date　　　　　　　Year

PICTURE STUDY

DICTATION

RHYMING WORDS

Write three words that rhyme with **dwell.**

Write three words that rhyme with **feed.**

DRAWING PAGE

from All People That on Earth Do Dwell

O enter then His courts with praise,
Approach with joy His courts unto;
Praise, laud, and bless His name always,
For it is seemly so to do.

For why? The Lord our God is good,
His mercy is forever sure;
His truth at all times firmly stood,
And shall from age to age endure.

—WILLIAM KETHE, 1561 (BASED ON PSALM 100)

Week 10 ♦ Day 1

Today is _____
                      Day   Date   Year

READ AND NARRATE

The Bear and the Bees
The Aesop for Children, illustrated by Milo Winter

Vocabulary to study before you read:

swarm	guessing	sharply
disappeared	destroy	injury
silence	provoke	rage

Draw a picture or series of pictures illustrating the story.

COPYBOOK

O enter then His courts with praise,

Approach with joy His courts unto;

Praise, laud, and bless His name always,

For it is seemly so to do.

ADDING SUFFIXES

Remember the rules for adding suffixes.

praise + *ing*	bless + *ed*	sure + *ly*
age + *ing*	do + *ing*	sure + *er*
little + *er*	mud + *y*	might + *y*

Week 10 • Day 2

Today is _____
          Day   Date   Year

NATURE STUDY

Choose a mammal, and talk about its characteristics, covering the points below. Sketch the mammal in the frame. Write the name of the mammal on the line below the frame.

- ❑ Its size
- ❑ Its body covering
- ❑ Its food
- ❑ Its means of protecting itself
- ❑ Its habits

COPYBOOK

For why? The Lord our God is good,

His mercy is forever sure;

His truth at all times firmly stood,

And shall from age to age endure.

PHONOGRAM OO

The phonogram **oo** *can say /oo/ as in* **food**, */oo/ as in* **book**, */ō/ as in* **floor**, *and /ŭ/ as in* **blood**.

Read these words, then copy them.

moon	good	door
loop	stood	flood
room	hood	crooked

Week 10 • Day 3

Today is _____
　　　　　　　Day　　　　　　　　　　Date　　　　　　　　　　Year

READ AND NARRATE

The Farmer and His Sons
The Aesop for Children, illustrated by Milo Winter

Vocabulary to study before you read:

bedside	heed	estate
generations	treasure	energy
search	harvest	profit
wealth	industry	

Draw a picture or series of pictures illustrating the story.

COPYBOOK

O enter then His courts with praise,

Approach with joy His courts unto;

Praise, laud, and bless His name always,

For it is seemly so to do.

For why? The Lord our God is good,

His mercy is forever sure;

His truth at all times stood,

And shall from age to age endure.

Week 10 • Day 4

Today is _____
　　　　　　　　　　Day　　　　　　　　　　　Date　　　　　　　　　　Year

PICTURE STUDY

DICTATION

RHYMING WORDS

Write three words that rhyme with **do.**

Write three words that rhyme with **good.**

DRAWING PAGE

FROM THE GOSPEL OF LUKE

Then the angel said to them, "Do not be afraid, for behold, I bring you good tidings of great joy which will be to all people. For there is born to you this day in the city of David a Savior, who is Christ the Lord. And this will be the sign to you: You will find a Babe wrapped in swaddling cloths, lying in a manger."

And suddenly there was with the angel a multitude of the heavenly host praising God and saying:

"Glory to God in the highest,
And on earth peace, goodwill toward men!"

—LUKE 2:10-14, NEW KING JAMES VERSION

Week 11 • Day 1

Today is _____
　　　　　　　　　Day　　　　　　　　　　　　　　　Date　　　　　　　　　　　　　　　Year

READ AND NARRATE

The Mouse and the Weasel
The Aesop for Children, illustrated by Milo Winter

Vocabulary to study before you read:

squeeze	narrow	tempting
determined	succeeded	gorged
satisfied	discomfort	anxiety
situation	sympathy	greediness

Draw a picture or series of pictures illustrating the story.

COPYBOOK

Then the angel said to them, "Do not be afraid, for behold, I bring you good tidings of great joy which will be to all people."

HOMONYMS

Homonyms are words that sound the same but have different spellings and meanings. **Dear** *and* **deer** *are homonyms.*

Write homonyms for the following words. Then, as an oral exercise with your teacher, use each word in a sentence to show you know what it means.

hear

sail

rode

won

mail

for

weak

Week 11 • Day 2

Today is _____
　　　　　　Day　　　　　　　Date　　　　　　　Year

NATURE STUDY

Choose a mammal, and talk about its characteristics, covering the points below. Sketch the mammal in the frame. Write the name of the mammal on the line below the frame.

- ❑ Its size
- ❑ Its body covering
- ❑ Its food
- ❑ Its means of protecting itself
- ❑ Its habits

COPYBOOK

"For there is born to you this day in the city of David a Savior, who is Christ the Lord. And this will be the sign to you: You will find a Babe wrapped in swaddling cloths, lying in a manger."

ADDING SUFFIXES

Remember the rules for adding suffixes.

wrap + ed	wrap + ing	swaddle + ing
sing + ing	be + ing + s	high + est
say + ing	peace + full	shine + y
praise + ing	clap + ed	sudden + ly

Week 11 • Day 3

Today is _____
              Day   Date   Year

READ AND NARRATE

The Milkmaid and Her Pail
The Aesop for Children, illustrated by Milo Winter

Vocabulary to study before you read:

shining	balanced	plans
mused	plenty	churn
hatching	business	scornfully
vanished	count	hatched

Draw a picture or series of pictures illustrating the story.

COPYBOOK

And suddenly there was with the angel a multitude of the heavenly host praising God and saying:

"Glory to God in the highest,
And on earth peace, goodwill toward men!"

MAKING PAST TENSE

Make these words past tense. Remember the rules you have learned.

say	praise	bring
is	find	swaddle
go	tell	sing

Week 11 • Day 4

Today is _____
                      Day   Date   Year

PICTURE STUDY

DICTATION

DAYS OF THE WEEK

Write the days of the week and their abbreviations.

DRAWING PAGE

Away in a Manger

Away in a manger, no crib for a bed,
The little Lord Jesus lay down His sweet head;
The stars in the bright sky looked down where He lay,
The little Lord Jesus, asleep on the hay.

The cattle are lowing, the baby awakes,
But little Lord Jesus no crying He makes;
I love thee, Lord Jesus! Look down from the sky,
And stay by my cradle till morning is nigh.

Be near me, Lord Jesus, I ask Thee to stay
Close by me forever, and love me, I pray;
Bless all the dear children in Thy tender care,
And fit us for heaven, to live with Thee there.

—TRADITIONAL CHRISTMAS CAROL

Week 12 • Day 1

Today is _____
   Day   Date   Year

READ AND NARRATE

Two Travelers and a Bear
The Aesop for Children, illustrated by Milo Winter

Vocabulary to study before you read:

company	safety	savage
snuffed	satisfied	whispered
desert	misfortune	friendship

Draw a picture or series of pictures illustrating the story.

COPYBOOK

Away in a manger, no crib for a bed,

The little Lord Jesus lay down His sweet head;

The stars in the bright sky looked down where He lay,

The little Lord Jesus asleep on the hay.

MAKING PAST TENSE

Make these words past tense. Remember the rules for adding suffixes.

look	sleep	low
make	love	awakes
stay	pray	live

Week 12 • Day 2

Today is _____
　　　　　　　Day　　　　　　　　Date　　　　　　　　Year

NATURE STUDY

Choose a mammal, and talk about its characteristics, covering the points below. Sketch the mammal in the frame. Write the name of the mammal on the line below the frame.

- ❑ Its size
- ❑ Its body covering
- ❑ Its food
- ❑ Its means of protecting itself
- ❑ Its habits

COPYBOOK

The cattle are lowing, the baby awakes,

But little Lord Jesus no crying He makes;

I love Thee, Lord Jesus! Look down from the sky,

And stay by my cradle till morning is nigh.

RHYMING WORDS

Write three words that rhyme with **lay**.

Write three words that rhyme with **sky**.

Write three words that rhyme with **bed**.

Week 12 • Day 3

Today is _____
       Day   Date   Year

READ AND NARRATE

The Hare and the Tortoise
The Aesop for Children, illustrated by Milo Winter

Vocabulary to study before you read:

mocking	prove	consented
judge	distance	ridiculous
slowly	steadily	goal
overtake	swift	

Draw a picture or series of pictures illustrating the story.

COPYBOOK

Be near me, Lord Jesus, I ask Thee to stay

Close by me forever, and love me, I pray;

Bless all the dear children in Thy tender care,

And fit us for heaven, to live with Thee there.

PHONOGRAMS EE AND EA

*The /ē/ sound can be made by both the **ee** and the **ea** phonograms.*

Read these words, then copy them.

thee	sleep	sheep
near	each	season
please	feed	reap

Week 12 • Day 4

Today is _____
  Day   Date   Year

PICTURE STUDY

DICTATION

HOMONYMS

Write the homonym for **dear.**

DRAWING PAGE

DRAWING PAGE

DRAWING PAGE

DRAWING PAGE

DRAWING PAGE

DRAWING PAGE

Made in United States
Troutdale, OR
12/21/2025